B405

DMUs COUNTRYWIDE

P. J. FOWLER

BRADFORD BARTON

Frontispiece: The 12.08 Bristol (Temple Meads) to Portsmouth, framed by the bridges of Sydney Gardens, Bath. No. B 405 is a Pressed Steel Co. set comprising Class 176 trailer No. W 59494, flanked by powered cars Nos. W 51342 (Class 117/2) and W 51384 (Class 117/1). [P. J. Fowler]

ISBN 0 85153 238 1

printed in Great Britain by H. E. Warne Ltd, London and St. Austell

for the publishers

D. BRADFORD BARTON LTD . Trethellan House . Truro . Cornwall . England

INTRODUCTION

Cinderella of modernisation in the 1950s, the diesel multiple-unit can now, in its maturity on British Railways, be viewed in perspective. Two interwoven lines of development emerged from common beginnings, although a related branch with a long history – the railbus – came to nothing. One line, the high-speed luxury diesel train, got going with the famous German 'Flying Hamburger' streamlined diesel unit of 1932. Introduction of the diesel-electric 'Blue Pullman' brought this idea to the travelling public in Britain during 1959, with its place being taken today by the High Speed Train. The other line came to prominence from 1954 to 1964, in the introduction of a fleet of nearly 5,000 diesel multiple-units to replace steam trains which were no longer economic to run, mostly on local and cross-country routes. Essentially, they were self-powered carriages, the concept for which was based not only on experiments but on experience at home and abroad. The units could be coupled together to form longer trains when needed, could carry out longer diagrams, were capable of fast turnrounds at terminal stations, and could be serviced readily. The snag in all this was the passenger. He soon found that the dmu did not entirely live up to the favourable image which was created for it in its early days; a slow suburban dmu packed at a peak time could be a hard place to ignore fumes, draughts, rattles, and a still indifferent ride – although he might be pleased to discover that he emerged cleaner than he would have from a steam train. Happily, some had fewer shortcomings, certain faults were corrected in others, and there was one notable redeeming feature for the interested passenger: he could now enjoy from either end of most units, a view of the approaching or receding track that had been denied him in locomotive-hauled trains.

Multiple-units are built in a substantial manner to sustain end-loadings which the low-powered railbus could not; the latter was so light in construction that it could not always be relied upon to operate track circuits. Its function has largely been assumed by the double-ended single-car multiple-unit, which will work with other units, run faster, and ride rather better. Most dmus employ a robust mechanical transmission from relatively small engines mounted under the floor, and their output is generally sufficient to avoid the need to power every car. There are a number of different seating arrangements for high or low density requirements. The units developed by the Southern Region depend on larger, slower-revving engines, which have electric transmission, but these engines cannot be mounted below the floor, and so take the place of some passenger seating. In the diesel Pullman trains, also, electric transmission was adopted, from engines in power cars – which had some passenger capacity – to those in non-driving motor cars. The 125 mph High-Speed Train is classified as a multiple-unit, but it may more correctly be regarded as a unit train whose formation is fixed for operating convenience. It has a single-ended diesel-electric locomotive at each end, one pushing, and one pulling, standard mk. 3 coaches. Formations are not coupled together to make trains of greater length.

The secondary-services dmu plan was master-minded at Derby, where about one third of the fleet was built. Private builders contributed about one half, in varied styles with some Derby influence. Swindon and the Southern Region demus make up the remainder. In any one railway location, there can be a misleading impression of lack of variety, whereas countrywide, quite the opposite is true. An exact coverage according to a distributional or geographical formula would be an unlikely achievement: the choice in this volume is a personal one, with a leaning towards Western Region material where it could illustrate certain aspects. Some of the fleet may be retired in the near future, just as some have already gone, although their passing has been less obvious than the disappearance of route mileage – some of which is recalled in this volume. Without the diesel multiple-unit, much more would have disappeared. A new generation is planned to replace the present one, and so these transports of delight will, in their turn, go on to join steam and a number of diesel locomotives which have been scrapped.

With or without the styling introduced later by industrial designers, the diesel multiple-unit train in its various forms for inter-urban, suburban, rural, or high-speed applications, is an interesting subject for the camera. I first came to appreciate seriously the photographic potential during a study of Bristol's last passenger branch, to Avonmouth and Severn Beach, a line worked mainly by single units. In compiling this volume, it has been a pleasure to examine the work which other photographers, too, have assembled, and to find that they also are discovering hitherto neglected possibilities.

In addition to the assistance of the contributors, I am grateful for the help kindly given by K. G. Barter, F. Bonneres, G. S. W. Calder, D. L. Davey, A. Featherstone, B. Haresnape, S. Hollier, A. D. McVean, D. Smart, J. A. M. Vaughan, and by the publisher and his staff. The guidance provided by John Howie has been invaluable, although the responsibility for accuracy remains mine.

P. J. Fowler

The GWR railcars were a step towards present-day diesel multiple-units. This one, supplied by AEC in 1940, could take up to a 60-ton trailing load—here an auto-coach trailer during disruption of normal services in the 1955 rail dispute. The photograph was taken west of Ebbw Junction, between Newport and Cardiff. Two single-ended power cars, with their under-floor engines and an existing corridor coach as the centre trailer, had an appearance not unlike a dmu of today, virtually pioneering the triple-car concept. [S. Rickard]

WELLINGTON
W 50071

Manchester-Blackpool services (among others) exploit the convenient way in which additional multiple-units can be coupled up to cope with extra demand. On this route, one three-car set may suffice at a slack period, with two sets as seen here being the normal provision. Occasionally, three sets, amounting to nine cars, may make up the train to meet a peak demand. [D. A. Flitcroft]

A Derby surburban dmu, new ex-works at Birmingham (Snow Hill) on 22 July 1957. The leading car, No. 50071, is now designated Class 116/2. Almost a 'Royal Train' turnout—except for the funny face scrawled on the nearest buffer. An admiring group of railwaymen on the platform had no eyes for the then-familiar GWR railcar No. 8, on its usual duty to Dudley via Swan Village. No. 8, like the other early railcars up to No. 17 inclusive, was not able to work in multiple with other vehicles. Its original cost was about £5,000. [P. J. Shoesmith]

Trailed behind a Swindon-built 'Cross-Country' dmu leaving Temple Meads station is a parcels van for Westbury in June 1968. These dmus were constructed to withstand a 100-ton end loading, more than enough for the extra vehicle; it would, however, affect the power to weight ratio. In contrast to the ultra-light railbus, the ability of the dmu to handle extra traffic confers added flexibility.
[P. J. Fowler]

Designed in the early 1950's, the 57 ft. two-car 'Derby lightweight' sets (now withdrawn from passenger service) were of necessity constructed integrally of light alloy, to make the best use of the low power ratings of diesel engines then available. Passenger accommodation was restricted, and the imposing 'cathedral' front, perhaps not easily built, was a source of reflections. As a possible accident hazard, it did not survive into later classes. Seen at Carlisle, this was a Whitehaven (mis-spelt) working in 1968. [J. G. Glover]

Its Rolls-Royce engines coping well with the rising gradients of the St. Pancras-Bedford route for which it was built, a Derby four-car set of 1959 bursts out into the sunshine as it speeds away from Elstree tunnel, led by Class 127 no. 51646. Cars with non-standard hydraulic transmission are distinguished by the red triangle coupling code. [Brian Morrison]

2C15
BEDFORD

Contrasting with the lines of a Class 52 diesel-hydraulic locomotive, and a Class 47 diesel-electric, is a Gloucester R C & W Co. 'Cross-Country' motor driving car. From the roof joint, the screen is raked forward above and ahead of the driver, then the front drops down over the control console. There is minimum loss of accommodation for passengers. Note, too, the much lower driving position of the dmu. [P. J. Fowler]

A Plymouth-based Gloucester R C & W Co. 'Cross-Country' set leaving Truro station in November 1974. Class 119/1 No. W 51079 (with 'tail' lamp) is leading a three-car set, the normal formation, operating the shuttle service to Falmouth. Units bearing the 'Blue Square' coding system have standard transmission and control mode, so can be coupled to work in multiple with others so marked, these being in a large majority. [Brian Morrison]

P588
A1

The Swindon 'Cross-Country' cab front has some flavour of the later Derby style, and strong links with that of the GWR railcar. Leading an Aberdeen to Inverness train entering Inverurie station during heavy rain early in 1974 is Class 120/1 motor brake composite No. SC 51785. Note that the seating accommodation of the 36-ton unit is quite limited, being only 34. With 'low density' seating layout, these sets were intended for the longer services, second class passengers enjoying two-a-side accommodation. This formation also included a suburban car, which has a higher-density layout. [Brian Morrison]

A Birmingham R C & W Co. dmu, with its characteristic straight-up cab front, between Silvertown and its rather grim North Woolwich terminus. Class 104/1 No. E 50547 leads, followed by Nos. E 59243 (Class 166 trailer) and E 50549 (Class 104/1 motor composite). Below, The Birmingham R C & W Co. sets introduced in 1961 for the West Riding-Manchester service over the Calder Valley route, have a smart appearance and improved power-to-weight ratio. This one is passing through Selby station *en route* to Manchester in June 1974. [Brian Morrison]

MANCHESTER

The 15.11 from Romford, a Cravens twin set led by Class 106 motor brake second No. 50369, arriving at Upminster against a brilliant August sky in 1973. These sets were introduced in 1956. [Brian Morrison]

Cravens Class 105/2 No. SC 51483 and Metro-Cammell Class 102/2 No. SC 51466—both motor brake seconds introduced in the same year, 1959—show their varied faces to the camera at Dundee (Tay Bridge), where they were respectively the 12.25 to Edinburgh and the 10.15 from Edinburgh, on 7 February 1974.

The product of master coach-builders, there is no mistaking a Cravens dmu, although the Swindon 'Cross-Country' cab front bears a likeness to it. This, another early set, formed a Welwyn to Kings Cross train, on Holloway bank.
[Brian Morrison]

An unusual view of a Metro-Cammell car, showing the distinctive effect brought about by unit-style window pans with bright aluminium surrounds. The clean roof line was achieved by raising the bodyside/roof junction and placing gutters only over doors. The unit is seen leaving Slaggyford for Haltwhistle in October 1973. Sadly, the future of this line is uncertain. [S. Creer]

York has a distinguished station, which is a celebrated example of railway architecture—here the stage for a four-car Metro-Cammell set in March 1975, forming the 16.35 Scarborough to Leeds train. Because of the experience of the manufacturer, there was little need for change in the design of these units all through their long production run. [M. H. C. Baker]

Introduced in 1959, the 'Blue Pullman' as it was originally called, was ahead of its time for style, comfort, and performance, for which passengers paid a supplementary fare. This westbound 'South Wales Pullman', in later grey and blue livery, was photographed at Patchway, Bristol, not long before withdrawal in mid-1973. Jumper leads for multiple control—a modification carried out on some cars—rather spoil the lines, which had been carefully developed from a number of mock-ups. [G. F. Gillham]

Many Western Region travellers at first mistook the High Speed Train for a new Pullman set when the prototype appeared on trial in late 1974. The HST, in its grey and blue livery, which extends from the power car at one end through the mk.3 prototype coaches to the power car at the other end, was seen in various parts of the region—here on a through road at Bristol (Temple Meads)—before entering service on 5 May 1975. The cab module, which differs a little in styling from the production version, is a glass-reinforced plastic moulding. [P. J. Fowler]

Scene of many photographs over the years before its closure following a protracted run-down, Birmingham (Snow Hill) with the London-bound eight-car 'Birmingham Pullman' standing at Platform 7 in a sunlit well at the south end, on 16 March 1962. The bodyside and end panels were painted medium blue, the windows enfolded in a cream band, and the roof (which joins the bodyside above its haunch, to the advantage of its styling) grey. Also included in the livery was a streamlined redesign of the Pullman coat-of-arms. Diesel-electric power cars drove traction motors in the train, which had air-conditioning supplied by auxiliary engines. [P. J. Shoesmith]

Among the most reliable diesel units on BR must surely be the Southern Region Class 205 3H 'Hampshire' diesel-electrics. They were introduced in 1957 on the Salisbury-Romsey-Portsmouth route, working a service of hourly trains with very few failures; No. 1103 accelerates away from Salisbury as the 09.45 for Portsmouth on 18 March 1975. [G. F. Gillham]

Southern Region diesel-electric sets are powered by a robust low-revving engine mounted above the floor, driving standard traction motors. A 3H 'Hampshire' demu set arrives at Hastings from Ashford in September 1971; beyond it in the sidings are 'Hastings' sets for the London service. [M. H. C. Baker]

Class 203 6B 'Hastings' cab, in close-up at Hastings, prior to departure of the unit for Tonbridge and Charing Cross. No. 1033 is one of the five sets to include a buffet car. Altogether, twenty six-car sets are in service, the not very lovely slab sides conforming to the loading gauge between Bexhill and Tunbridge Wells. 'Hastings' units with an added full-width driving trailer have a curious appearance, which has caused them to be known as 'Tadpoles'.
[M. H. C. Baker]

The first 'Hastings' units were put together from adapted short-frame coaches to a restricted width, but later versions were purpose-built 64 ft. 6 ins long on standard BR underframes. Two of the later sets, Nos. 1012 and 1034, speed through the Wiltshire countryside near Wilton with the Saturdays-only 13.50 Exeter-Brighton, which 'Hastings' units have worked from May 1972. A hatch on the leading car allows its engine—much larger than those mounted underfloor in diesel-mechanical types—to be lifted through the roof.
[G. F. Gillham]

Rather more handsome, a 1962 Class 207 3D 'East Sussex' set, on the hourly Hastings-Ashford run via Rye, seen leaving Ore, Hastings. The power car—with an English Electric 600 bhp engine—is nearer the camera, on track which has a third rail to give a head shunt into and out of Hastings emu depot.
[P. W. Robinson]

The curves in the 'Trans-Pennine' cab styling were made possible by designing the cab as a moulding in glass-reinforced plastic. This approach contributed to the high structural strength of these sets, and their high power-to-weight ratio, needed for the steeply graded Hull-Leeds-Manchester cross-country route.
[D. Griffiths]

High on any list of the most attractive sights on BR metals must be Swindon's 'Trans-Pennine' sets, introduced in 1960, a date which came late enough to allow adequate consideration to be given to the aesthetic qualities of the design. One of the type is approaching Selby station with an early morning train on 15 May 1973, working through from Hull to Liverpool. [J. H. Cooper-Smith]

At Dean, south of Salisbury, leading car No. W 52095 of an 'Inter-City' set approaches on a fine April day in 1968. This type operated between Cardiff and Portsmouth in 1967 and 1968. Built at Swindon with stressed bodies to be light, yet meet main-line standards, their appearance—aided by wrap-around windows in the cab—is attractive notwithstanding the presence of a corridor connection. There is much in common with 'Cross-Country' vehicles, excepting the heavier underframe end fitted with centre buckeye couplers, together with buffing, drawgear, and gangways as fitted to standard coaches, and 'Inter-City' cars meet the main-line requirement of 200-tons compressive strength. [G. F. Gillham]

Car No. W 50862—a Derby suburban type adapted to carry parcels traffic, designated Class 130—heads a westbound train of parcels vehicles through Sonning cutting on 27 April 1974. [Brian Morrison]

Provided with gangway connections and a cab at either end for operation as a single unit, a Gloucester R C & W Co. Class 128 motor parcels van makes its way along the electrified Euston line, passing Marston Green golf course, on the eastern boundary of Birmingham. The parcels vans, small in number, find a niche where there is not the capacity or station time for other trains to lift parcels traffic. [P. J. Shoesmith]

A double-ended Pressed-Steel Co. unit with seating for 65 passengers, Class 121 No. 55031 at Twyford, where it is about to leave for Henley-on-Thames on a Sunday afternoon in July 1973. The Henley-on-Thames branch was the scene of the initial Automatic Warning System (AWS) experiments, which led to greater safety for all trains equipped with it. **[Brian Morrison]**

The Bridport branch survived until 1975, worked latterly by diesel single units. Pressed Steel Co. car No. 55033 is standing in Bridport station,at the end of the 9¼-mile branch from Maiden Newton, in Dorset, in March 1975. The branch, which once extended some way further to West Bay, closed two months later. [P. Clark]

Single units can be used to boost the power-to-weight ratio (and passenger capacity) of a three car set. A Pressed Steel Co. double-ended unit, at the rear of a Swindon 'Cross-Country' triple, assists in the seven-mile grind up from Severn Tunnel to Patchway—mostly 1 in 100—in July 1970. [P. J. Fowler]

Seen through the arch of a farm bridge still filled with wartime anti-tank obstacles, this single unit is a workman's special beside the Kennet & Avon Canal, on the Western Region main line, between Bedwyn and Crofton. Several singles are assigned to departmental stock for such duties. [T. G. Flinders]

The Severn Estuary and Wales lie beyond Pressed Steel Co. Class 121 No. 55033, approaching from Severn Beach as it motors towards Avonmouth in bright winter sunshine on 29 January 1974. It was bound for Bristol (Temple Meads), through the Avon Gorge, and Clifton Down tunnel, a branch line route whose survival has been aided by paytrain operation. Development of the Temple Meads area, and urban transport problems, should now work to the advantage of this line. [P. J. Fowler]

On weekends, diesel multiple units are often found operating enthusiasts' excursions to forgotten corners of the railway system. In April 1972, the L C G B 'Somerset Quarry Rambler' special was an 'Inter-City' dmu, not far from 'home' in Wiltshire, at Westlecot Manor, between Swindon junction and Swindon (Town).
[T. G. Flinders]

Not only enthusiasts, but the travelling public too, enjoy the view through the driver's cab. Here it includes a Derby-built Class 116, once the standard suburban type on routes from Birmingham (Snow Hill), though now they appear anywhere in the Birmingham area. This one is in their original territory, just south of Acock's Green, on the line to Leamington Spa. Hourly off-peak trains normally cross near Lapworth, so it is likely that the approaching train is a peak-hour addition for Leamington or Stratford-on-Avon via Bearley. [P. J. Shoesmith]

Three Birmingham R C & W Co. suburban triple sets, forming a 'last day' special train, pick their way through the undergrowth of the Newbury-Welford Park freight-only branch on 3 November, 1973. Passenger services had been withdrawn in 1960. [G. F. Gillham]

SPECIAL
B2

SPECIAL

Some early units have been converted from revenue-earning passenger service to other duties. This 1957 lightweight set, made by Gloucester R C & W Co., is now included in departmental stock and is used as an engineer's inspection special. On its right, in May 1974, is Class 08 No. 3381 (now 08/311), shunting Castleford yard. [J. G. Glover]

The General Manager's saloon—a Wickham two-car set once Nos. E 50416/E 51171, respectively motor brake and driving trailer. Specially refurbished some ten years after it was first placed in service, it is now numbered DB 975005/DB 975006 in departmental stock, and is here entering Norwich station—the immaculate finish sparkling in the East Anglian sunshine—on 26 June 1975. The motor brake is leading. [Brian Morrison]

Shuttle services might have been made for the multiple-unit train, because of the driving cab at either end. A Cravens leads a Gloucester R C & W Co. car at Braintree, in August 1971, on the Braintree-Witham line, a basically commuter line which is being electrified. [G. R. Mortimer]

Only a few steps from Woodside pier on the River Mersey was Birkenhead (Woodside), a celebrated small-scale 'Paddington' across the river from its more successful LNWR competitor, Liverpool (Lime Street). Unloading in this northernmost part of the former GWR system in August 1967 is a Park Royal Class 103/145 set.
[P. J. Shoesmith]

Now modestly improved into a local railhead, without the loss of its country atmosphere, Castle Cary on the West of England main line was visited regularly only by cross-country trains to Weymouth, and still relied on gas-lamps for lighting, at the time of this photograph in August 1972. Trains for Weymouth, such as this set which has been divided at Westbury from a portion for Salisbury, stop at Castle Cary and then leave the main line, branching left for the south just beyond the station after having taken a single-line key from an instrument on the down platform.

[P. J. Fowler]

The single-line electric key-token instrument at Castle Cary station. This is a double-release instrument, connected to another in the signal box at Castle Cary; the section controlled is to Yeovil (Pen Mill). Much of the mileage covered by dmus is on single lines.

[P. J. Fowler]

The signalman at Swavesey about to make an exchange with the driver of the 09.44 St. Ives to Cambridge train on 2 October 1970. The pouch on a heavy ring aided the operation in the steam age, but was found to cause damage in diesel cabs. This line is now open only for freight, having been closed to passenger traffic on the following day, 3 October. [G. R. Mortimer]

An exchange on the move demands careful coordination, by both participants. The driver of a Weymouth to Bristol train has just put the key into the waiting hand of the signal man, as the Class 117 suburban unit comes off the single line branch from Yeovil, and continues forward on the main line into Castle Cary station, which is just out of sight to the left. Note that the comparatively low driving position facilitates the exchange. [P. J. Fowler]

At a quick glance an everyday triple set perhaps, but Derby class 108 power cars are more commonly found alone with a trailer in twin sets. The two lightweight power cars with a centre trailer are leaving the fishing village of Robin Hood's Bay in June 1962. The coastal journey from Scarborough to Whitby—where this morning train for Middlesbrough would have a reversal—led across valleys running to the sea. At Robin Hood's Bay, a descent at 1 in 39 from Flyingdales changed to a 1 in 43 climb; one can almost hear the rasp of the exhaust as the unit pulls away.

[P. J. Shoesmith]

B6

A triple set sheds the accumulated effects of a heavy rain shower at Cardiff (General), as it moves away on a Sunday afternoon in 1967, for a rather sleepy journey on the north bank of the River Severn to Gloucester (Central). The white roof panel over the cab quickly became discoloured, and fell from favour. [P. J. Fowler]

The low mid-winter sun picks out the 15.18 Bristol (Temple Meads) to Portsmouth (Harbour) demu (SR Class 3H), followed by the camera as it speeds towards Bath in January 1975. [P. J. Fowler]

A Newcastle to Middlesborough (via Sunderland) dmu leans away in the curve, as it gets under way in front of an elevated signal box at Billingham-on-Tees in 1966. The Derby lightweight set includes a Metro-Cammell trailer (second coach). The track condition is emphasised by a telephoto lens.
[J. A. M. Vaughan]

Funicular-style, single units by Pressed Steel cross below Clifton Down station, Bristol, in August 1974. Delayed by late running of the 18.10 Temple Meads-Severn Beach unit, which has come up from Redland station on a singled section at 1 in 76, the 18.00 reverse working (left) eases away from level, back down the gradient at the end of the passing loop. [P. J. Fowler]

A long telephoto lens creates a striking impression of a St. Pancras-bound Derby dmu at speed on the main line between Radlett and Elstree. The provision of a door for each seating bay, clearly seen here, speeds passenger movement at stations but encourages draught and vibration problems. [P. A. Dobson]

2C04
BEDFORD

The constricted approach above street level to St. Pancras station, built boldly on a difficult site, must benefit from the advantage of the dmu that it can be driven from either end, which allows it to enter and leave smartly at termini, without light engine movements. Derby-built Class 127 No. M 51642 leads a four-car set away at 12.45 on a journey to Bedford (Midland Road) in March 1975. [Brian Morrison]

One of the frequent Derby units for Luton, under the remarkable arch at St. Pancras. The Victorian hotel, now converted to offices, and the terminal buildings, are tributes to the age which built them, if less daring than the iron arch above, which spans 240′ and is tensioned by the floor girders of the station itself. [M. H. C. Baker]

The classical 5:1 ratio arch, in miniature, of the little wood-and-iron station at Banbury (Merton Street), albeit without glass. Steps were provided for passengers to ascend or descend between the platform and early-style Derby lightweight cars. The cars were modified to operate as singles along this branch from Verney Junction, on the Oxford-Bletchley-Bedford-Cambridge line. The service was quite good—seven up trains on weekdays, three through to Bletchley, four to Buckingham. This unit was a departure for Bletchley, in October 1959. Not all has to remain just a memory, for one became a departmental unit, No. DB 975010.
[P. J. Shoesmith]

Not far from the Glamorgan coast, a Barry Island to Merthyr regular interval train, a Derby suburban set bearing yellow warning flashes and end roof panels which are still all-white, emerges from Cogan tunnel—between Dinas Powis and Cogan—in April 1964. Destinations alternate, so the next train would normally run to Treherbert. In summer, the traffic along here between Cardiff and Barry can be very heavy. The signal box controlled access to the relief goods line, since lifted. [S. Rickard]

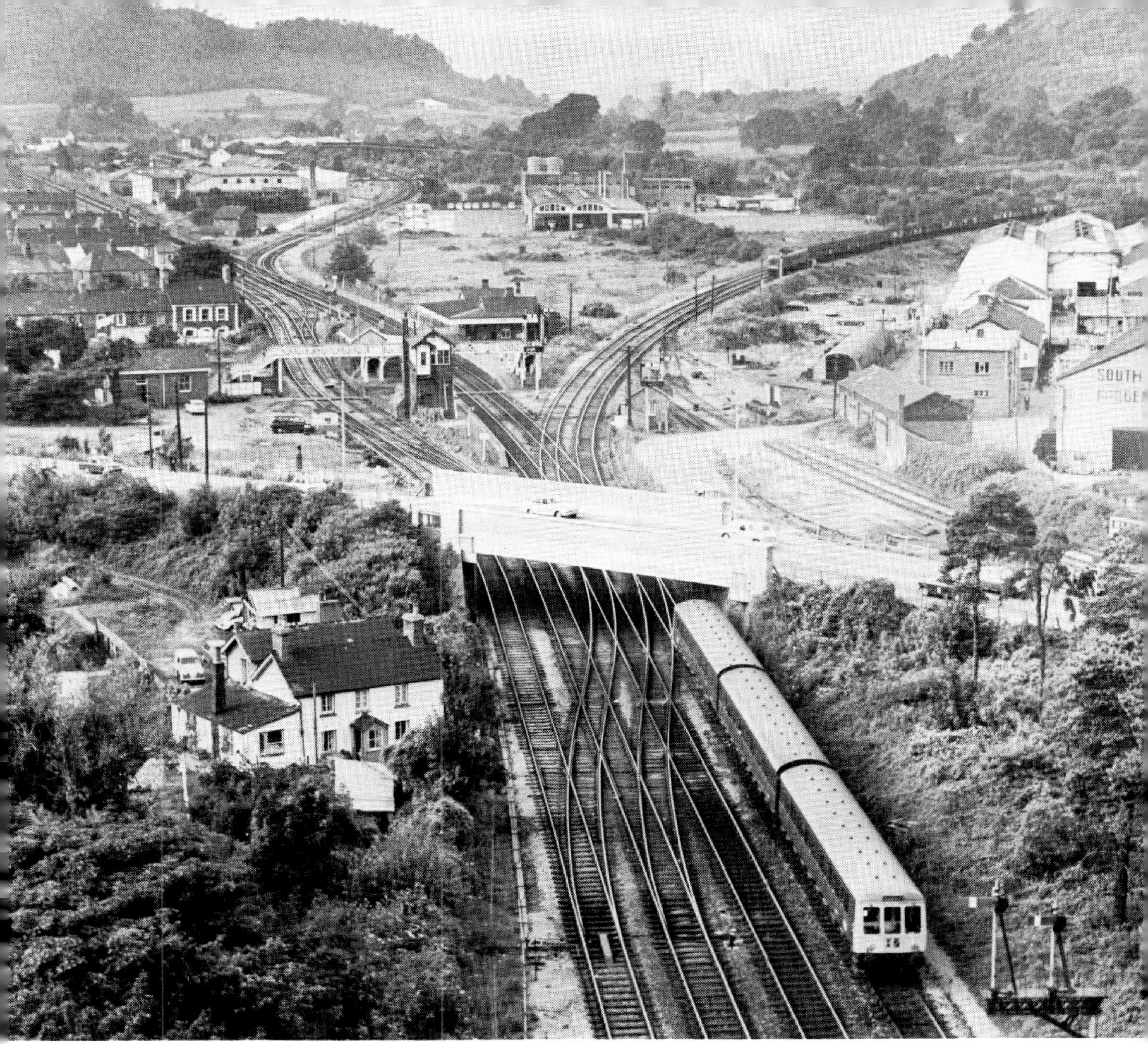

Trains from the South Wales valleys nowadays funnel towards Cardiff. A suburban set has just passed through the now modernised station at Taff's Well, on its way from Treherbert, at the head of the Rhondda Valley, to Cardiff and Barry. The trains are well-patronised, run frequently, and give main-line connections at Cardiff (Central), formerly Cardiff (General), as well as convenient bus transfers. The view from Walnut Tree viaduct, which carried the one-time Barry Railway over the Taff Vale main line, provided striking views, including on this occasion a coal train on the line from Caerphilly. [P. J. Fowler]

B2

mid the all-pervasive
ate of Blaenau
estiniog stands a
erby
ghtweight-alloy twin
et forming the 09.30
r Llandudno, on 24
ıly 1969. Blaenau
estiniog stands
npressively grim and
ey at the head of the
anch from
andudno Junction,
d was one of the
ost prosperous
wns in North Wales
hen the slate industry
as at its height. The
e continues left: at
e time it went to Bala
nction, but now it
rves the occasional
eds of a nuclear
wer station at
awsfynydd.
[G. F. Gillham]

The journey of about
one hour duration
between Llandudno
and Blaenau Ffestiniog
has a basically three
hour frequency. On a
bright April day in
1974, Derby and
Metro-Cammell
twin-sets together
make up a Blaenau
Ffestiniog to
Llandudno train, which
is descending the
upper slopes of the
Lledr Valley towards
Roman Bridge. This
was a Beeching
closure but is now
open again as an
unstaffed halt.
[A. W. Hobson]

The LNWR opened the Caernarvon branch (from the Chester-Holyhead line at Menai Bridge) in the 1850's, and BR closed it to passenger traffic in 1970. On track now lifted, a Park Royal twin-set (driving trailer composite and motor brake second) is approaching Caernarvon from Llandudno. The Menai Straits and Anglesey lie in the distance. [A. W. Hobson]

When the fleet of Blue Square coded Park Royal, Derby, Metro-Cammell, and—for a while—Cravens and Gloucester twins, was introduced into North Wales in 1965, the incompatible Yellow Diamond coded early Derby lightweight units on branch lines were transferred away. Here, in May 1962, an early Derby twin, made up of cars M 79185 and M 79190, continues south from Caernarvon—with the one-time garrison town's castle just beyond—on a journey from Bangor to Pwllheli. [Michael Messenger]

The 10.54 Pwllheli-Machynlleth train, strengthened to two Metro-Cammell twin units for the remaining Saturday holiday traffic on 23 September 1972, leaving Penhelig Halt, one of the two stations in Aberdovey, the other being Aberdovey station itself, one mile away. Determined local support has kept the Cambrian Coast line open.
[A. W. Hobson]

Units deployed on the lonely Central Wales line, normally two-car Swindon sets with both cars powered, have for some time been fitted with a beamed headlight at each end for greater safety at night, especially on level crossings. This unusual photograph, taken early in the morning at Pontardulais, shows the 05.50 Swansea to Shrewsbury, the first train of the day, approaching the now unstaffed halt on 24 April 1970. Subsequent demolition of the station buildings has underlined the decline of this once grand junction, where the LNWR Swansea (Victoria) line met the GWR Llanelly to Llandilo route.
[J. A. M. Vaughan]

The 16.16 Machynlleth-Pwllheli train, running as a six-car Metro-Cammell formation on a weekday at the end of July 1970, stops at Porthmadog on the Cambrian Coast line. In recent years, Metro-Cammell units have become regular performers on North Wales lines.
[G. F. Gillham]

Carrying a good trade in earlybird commuters—including some railwaymen—the 06.55 Swindon to Bristol (Temple Meads) is comfortably filled as it picks up speed beside the River Avon after a stop at Keynsham. It is worked variously by 'Cross-Country' or suburban sets, and latterly sometimes a Metro-Cammell unit now some are based at Bristol. On arrival at Temple Meads it becomes the 08.09 for Cardiff, but is not advertised as a through train. [P. J. Fowler]

For many, the view from the spectacular one-time atmospheric railway along the South Devon sea wall is likely to be that from a train such as the Class 50 – hauled 09.55 Paignton to Paddington, pausing at Dawlish in June 1975. Dmus on local trips provide a more lingering look, with their greater number of stops, giving day visitors in summer access to long beaches. The dmu making its call at Dawlish is the 10.05 from Exeter (St. Davids) to Newton Abbot and is made up of two Derby sets based at Plymouth, Nos. P 357/355—with a Metro-Cammell composite trailer in the leading triple set.
[P. J. Fowler]

Derby suburban set No. P 357, with Metro-Cammell trailer and now running as one triple set, forms an additional Exeter to Newton Abbot train on 11 June 1975. It has emerged from a short tunnel out of Dawlish and is passing the wind-sculpted red sandstone cliffs of Coryton Cove. Less cruel than those on the North Devon coast, winter seas are nevertheless savage enough to lead to high maintenance costs, which must be borne if this busy line, the only rail link with Cornwall and much of Devon, is to be kept open.
[P. J. Fowler]

Passengers and baggage on the 13.35 from Exeter seemed to be crammed into every available space of Pressed Steel Co. single unit No. 55029 on 3 April 1969, and are extricating themselves—no doubt thankfully—on arrival at Okehampton. [G. F. Gillham]

A Minehead-Taunton train at Crowcombe on the West Somerset line in August 1968. Crowcombe is nine miles from Taunton. The full twenty-five mile journey took one hour, which was no better than it had been by steam. [P. W. Robinson]

A three-car 'Cross-Country' set built by Gloucester R C & W Co., bearing down on Stogumber in West Somerset, where the wooden boards of the station are hot in the sunshine of a West Country summer. It was the 14.45 Taunton-Minehead, in July 1970, a few months before closure. Re-opening of this branch as a preserved line should prove to be an outstanding attraction. [G. F. Gillham]

A Leeds to Manchester train, worked by a 'Trans-Pennine' set, emerging from the south end of Morley Tunnel, which is nearly two miles long—a ventilation shaft can be seen on the skyline—and situated between Leeds and Huddersfield. The NER pushed through this route, which is now a candidate for electrification, because they were sure of substantial new business. Diesel multiple-units were chosen for it because the extra locomotives which otherwise would have been needed would not only have been under-utilised at night, but their first costs, with rolling stock, were expected to be greater.

[J. H. Cooper-Smith]

Ten Metro-Cammell sets, based at Leeds (Neville Hill) depot, fitted with experimental four-character head-code boxes. O set fitted in this wa seen here approach Sowerby Bridge station in Septemb 1974, working the 11.10 (normally 11. Manchester (Victori to Leeds over the Calder Valley route, Bradford. During engineering work i Summit Tunnel, departures were fiv minutes earlier tha usual, due to the increased journey time. Birmingham & W Co. 'Calder Va dmus are customa performers, but Metro-Cammells ar even Cravens from Hull are seen.

[D. Griffi

Shortened 'Trans-Pennine' sets are not uncommon. Another five-car set—originally six—makes up the 12.10 Liverpool-York train on 14 August 1973, here near the summit of the 15-mile climb out from Manchester on Saddleworth viaduct. The gradient, which is severe in the early stages at 1 in 59 and 1 in 47, eases considerably to 1 in 175 at Saddleworth.

[D. A. Flitcroft]

Birmingham R C & W Co. units appear on most of the well-patronised and basically half-hourly Manchester (Victoria)-Blackpool trains. Four Class 104 power cars and two Class 169 trailers make up a Blackpool train, passing Kearsley power station in September 1973. They also run many Southport services, as well as turning up on locals. Some diagrams cover trips to both Blackpool and Southport—for example, the 18.15 from Blackpool covers the 20.00 Manchester (Victoria) to Southport. [D. A. Flitcroft]

Many services on the steeply-graded lines around Manchester are operated with Cravens units. In a attractive heather-covered cutting near Bolton, Nos. M 50787 and M 50754, with some 600 bhp for a short-frame twin-set (both cars powered) are about 700′ above sea level, just before a descent through Sough Tunnel to Darwen and Blackburn. [D. A. Flitcroft]

A Carlisle to Whitehaven train in 1974, formed by a pair of Derby lightweight twin-sets, rolls along past Derwent and Moss Bay steel works, Workington. In each case, the Class 142 driving trailer is leading a Class 108 motor brake second. Safety bars over windows in doors can just be seen. The industrial diesel on the left is one built by the Yorkshire Engine Co. [P. W. Robinson]

The interested observer at the south end of Wolverhampton (Low Level)—ex-GWR—in 1964, was most likely hoping for a steam locomotive to head his way. However, the occasional passage of a dmu from the Burton-on-Trent and Walsall line, towards Wolverhampton (High Level)—ex LMS—would provide for him a picture very typical of lines in the 'Black Country'. Here the twin 57 ft. bodies of a Metro-Cammell unit, sporting a yellow warning panel below the cab windows, work the service on 10 April. The lining-out, with three cream bands, of the original livery, is clearly visible. [P. J. Shoesmith]

Keswick No. 1 signa box frames a Class 142 Derby lightweight driving trailer, leading a Class 108/2 powered car, which are waiting at Keswick to form the 15.30 to Penrith, on 19 February 1972, just two weeks before closure. The Workington-Keswick section closed in 1966, and the remaining part of the line was reduced about two years later to single token working. The Kingmoor-based later sets had replaced the earlier pattern Derby lightweights, based at Carlisle Upperby, in 1969, when the earlier type was withdrawn. [G. J. Jackson]

A Class 108/2 Derby lightweight and Class 142 trailer leave Troutbeck for Keswick as the 12.10 from Penrith, in the wintry sunshine of February 1972; exhaust from the trailer comes from its heating system. Skiddaw towers over this scenically magnificent line, which continued in a descent to the Lakeland terminus.
[G. J. Jackson]

In a Pennine setting near Slaggyford on a warm July day, a Metro-Cammell unit makes an irregular and infrequent journey up from Haltwhistle to Alston, a well-known touring centre, on 7 July 1973. [J. H. Cooper-Smith]

Scottish 'Land Cruises' by dmu enjoyed great popularity and were notable for their offering a remarkably varied collection of vehicles. The 'Six Lochs' Land Cruise, on Easter Monday 1963, brought together Gloucester R C & W Co., Metro-Cammell, and Cravens cars, here seen entering Killin station from the Loch Tay shed line. Ben Lawers is beyond them, in stirring scenery which can no longer be enjoyed in this manner. [S. Rickard]

403
0L
G

Busy Glasgow Central's wires above it, a Cravens two-car set, made up of Class 105/2 motor brake second No. SC 51484 and Class 141 driving trailer composite No. SC 56473, moves out into the November sunshine of 1973 wit the 10.40 local to Lanark via Uddingstone.
[Brian Morrison

Awesome in its size and conception, the largest cantilever bridge of the nineteenth century effortlessly carries across the Firth of Forth two twin Gloucester Class 100/Class 143 sets, forming the 13.50 Edinburgh (Waverley) to Cowdenbeath, on a misty Saturday in August 1970. A number of these units were deployed in the Edinburgh area, based at Leith Central depot. Progressive phasing out for standardisation took place in the early 1970's. Two sets found their way to the North Yorkshire Moors Railway, which has overhauled them to work between Goathland and Pickering. [G. J. Jackson]

Edinburgh (Waverley)—formerly North British—where a local for Thornton Junction, near Kirkcaldy, is waiting on 21 July 1961; the Metro-Cammell unit bears a visibility flash, which was changed to larger yellow areas when it was found to be insufficiently conspicuous. The early 1960's was a period of decline for local services. Along Princes Street, the former Caledonian station was closed, and Waverley absorbed those services which remained. Most of the dmu mileage now is on main lines. The station occupies a remarkable site between fashionable Princes Street—in the background—and Edinburgh Castle. [S. Rickard]

Dmus were seen on the Waverley route, but severe gradients helped to make the experiments short-lived, and although the enthusiast was unwilling to accept it, these were the last years of the first railway across the border. In an atypically gentle setting, a Gloucester set leaves Melrose, on its way from Edinburgh (Waverley) to Hawick in July 1967. [C. J. M. Lofthus]

A Metro-Cammell triple set with four-character headcode box, crosses the River Aire as the 10.57 Leeds to Morecambe train. In this early autumn scene near Gargrave, the Pennine Way flanks the distant hills, meeting the railway farther on at Bell Busk. [T. G. Flinders]

A Derby twin 64 ft.-car set, Classes 114/148, led by the motor brake second, runs across a masonry bridge over the River Nidd, leaving Knaresborough. It was the 10.15 from York to Harrogate. The additional full-length window is a distinguishing point from the 57 ft. lightweights. [S. Creer]

Referred to as "the other Clapham Junction" when the line to Tebay via Ingleton was operating, Clapham Junction in North Yorkshire is—unlike its namesake—very isolated. Two of the 1961 Birmingham R C & W Co. sets arrive in June 1974, on a Leeds-Morecambe working. [S. Creer]

The 51 supports for the Kent viaduct bear a pair of Derby lightweight twins over to Arnside, on a Barrow to Preston run on a still and rather overcast morning in June 1974. The comparatively fragile light alloy construction of these units renders them prone to accident damage, especially if they encounter a vehicle which is more heavily built. This is reflected in their not being permitted to take a trailing load heavier than a four-wheeled van (17 tons), having, in any case, limited power. [S. Creer]

Despite planned maintenance, improvisation may be called for. On 6 September 1969, the 11.43 Weymouth to Oxford train—a suburban dmu—experienced great difficulty in climbing to Evershot summit. The station staff at Yeovil (Pen Mill) are replenishing the failing unit's overheated radiator from a watering-can. [J. A. M. Vaughan]

One of the best-known of all locations for railway photography is Sonning Cutting. A Pressed Steel Co. suburban set from Paddington to Didcot is in company with a Paddington to Oxford train, a fast-moving Swindon Inter-City dmu, in July 1970. When they ceased to operate between Cardiff and Portsmouth, 'Inter-City' types were transferred to the Oxford route, and some more powerful seven-car sets were formed, each from two four-car sets by removal of a trailer. Threes and fours also run. Their career on London outer-suburban services was more successful than it had previously been.

Car No. S 60803 leads a Class 205 3H 'Hampshire' dmu slowly over the River Avon, just getting under way propelled by an unseen motor driving car, after a stop at Bradford-on-Avon station. The type has been familiar for several years on services from Portsmouth through to Bristol, such as this, the 12.56 from Portsmouth (Harbour) on 22 July 1974. The full cross-country journey takes about three hours, and is a necessary if not over-remunerative service, with a strong seasonal element. [P. J. Fowler]

Problems, problems; the 3H 'Hampshire' unit occupying the up main line at Keynsham is the 06.50 Bristol (Temple Meads) to Portsmouth (Harbour), which has been held back for some 80 minutes, due to a rail break before Bath. The 06.55 Swindon to Bristol 'Cross-Country' unit has brought the pilotman from Bath, to send the 3H unit, and the rest of the queue which stretched back into Bristol, forward wrong line to Bath.
[P. J. Fowler]

As a blizzard in March 1975 lifts a little, a Metro-Cammell triple set clears Summit Tunnel, 2809 yards long, and situated between Rochdale and Todmorden. This is the high point on the Manchester-Bradford-Leeds main line via the Calder Valley. [D. A. Flitcroft]

Despite an overnight snowfall which had been so heavy that it not only blocked road access to Bristol for some hours, but almost immobilised internal transport, the morning Pullman from Paddington—its slipstream drawing a cloud of loose snow at St. Annes Park station—made a punctual journey to Temple Meads on 8 December 1968. There was an added minor touch of drama due to the presence of the Duchess of Kent, who was arriving for an important civic engagement and had boarded the train when her flight was cancelled. [P. J. Fowler]

Not a test bed for dmus, but an automatic washer applying a spray of water following a scrub with cleaning solution. Getting a routine wash with its windows firmly closed at Victoria Park, Bristol, in May 1973 is a Birmingham R C & W Co. high-density suburban type, set No. B 478. [P. J. Fowler]

On part of the original Severn Valley line, a Gloucester R C & W Co. single unit—the afternoon Hartlebury to Bewdley train—pauses in a snowstorm at Stourport-on-Severn, in February 1969. Dmu heating was troublesome at first, but reliability improved with the adoption of more robust equipment.
[J. G. Glover]

Set No. B 478 again, comprising cars numbered W 51307/59474/51322, in the servicing bay at Marsh Junction (Bristol) in 1975. Refuelling, lubrication, and minor repairs are carried out here. On the whole, dmus are sturdy, reliable workhorses which do not suffer many disabling failures. Types with a good record will continue in service for a long time yet. [P. J. Fowler]

In Lochgorm depot, Inverness, during March 1974, is a Swindon 'Cross-Country' dmu – Nos. SC 51793/59683/51789 – alongside Class 24/1 locomotive No. 5130 (Now No. 24 130). Each power car of the unit has two British United Traction (BUT) ''A'' type underfloor engines. Prominent on the side of the engine lying in the foreground is the fluid flywheel. Next is the exhaust manifold (incomplete) above the cylinders, then the air compressor (far side), fuel lines, governor and shutdown solenoid, tachometer generator, and belt drive for the fan unit. [Brian Morrison]

6

Perhaps the best time of all for station photography is at night, the hours of darkness being very rewarding for those with patience and a tripod. The station lighting at Leamington Spa illuminates a Gloucester R C & W Co. Class 128 motor parcels van, drawn up for loading on 1 December 1970. [P. J. Shoesmith]

Evening at Salisbury station: on the left is Class 205 3H No. 1111, forming the 21.31 to Reading; beside it is a Gloucester triple set, Class 119/1 motor brake composite No. 51062 leading, on the 19.50 Bristol to Portsmouth. [G. F. Gillham]

For a visit to Leeds in July 1974, the refurbished Metro-Cammell dmu carried the 'WY' motif of the West Yorkshire Passenger Transport Executive. This area is one where British Rail have hopes for cooperation by local authorities in schemes which would improve the standards of existing vehicles. The "Facelift"—to some extent an interim measure to bridge the gap to the next generation—can be at various levels to match the financial participation. A reduction in noise levels and fumes, together with a cheerful welcome for the passenger in the interior decor, will work wonders where it is necessary.
[J. G. Glover]

The suburban dmu is a way of life in South Wales. There, the reopening of some stations and lines once closed has been under active consideration. For example, Barry, which is presently served only from Cardiff, strongly merits resumption of passenger services to and from Bridgend. The photograph shows a Derby Class 116/2 leading a three-car set out of Porthkerry tunnel on 25 July 1959, this being the 11.09 Bridgend to Barry train, prior to closure of this portion to passenger traffic. [S. Rickard]

HighSpeed Trains—"Inter-City 125"—are poles apart from the humbler units with which they are classified, but they have in common the important facility for being driven from either end. To match their modern image, some station remodelling has taken place, although large changes may have to wait to be combined with possible future electrification. The prototype High Speed Train—less "Sharp" in appearance than production units—operated an 07.45 to Paddington from Bristol (Parkway), during closure of the Badminton route in mid-1975 for upgrading to high-speed running. The only intermediate stop—seen here—was at Bristol Stapleton Road. [P. J. Fowler]